Bootsie

The King

MIKE JAMES

Text copyright © Mike James 2011
ISBN: 9781921787492
Published by Vivid Publishing
P.O. Box 948, Fremantle
Western Australia 6959
www.vividpublishing.com.au

Chapters

1

The Season's Over

"We should have beaten them last week," Bootsie said to Mr Butkiss as they stood on the sidelines and watched the Grand Final game between the Central Cobras and the South West Storm. The Cobras had knocked out the Hornets in the semi-final and Bootsie was keen to see how they would fare against the Storm. He was still bitter about their loss to the Cobras and felt that the Hornets could have beaten them, but for some reason the Cobras always seemed to have it over the Hornets and he couldn't work out why.

"They were simply the better team on the day, that's all," said Mr Butkiss.

Bootsie had come to the game with Mr Butkiss and his son Chris. Bootsie and Chris had become quite good friends and Bootsie had taken Chris under his wing to help him along in his first season playing rugby. Chris was a natural athlete and would probably be good at any sport he tried; he had very good balance which any good sportsman needs.

When the full time whistle blew, the Central Cobras had won the Grand Final *again*. The score was 21 to 19.

"That was a great game," Bootsie said to Mr Butkiss from the backseat of his old car on the way home.

"I think we had the goods to beat either of the teams today," replied Mr Butkiss. "It's a shame about last week. Oh' well, next year maybe," he added.

"That's it then, the season's over," said Bootsie.

"Next season, you'll see Bootsie, we'll get to the grand final," replied his coach.

"I sure hope so Mr Butkiss, I sure hope so," he replied.

"Let's just have a break over the summer, then we'll come back and focus on winning the Grand Final next season. We took some pretty big steps this season don't forget," added Mr Butkiss.

They dropped Bootsie home and he waited out the front of his house until Mr Butkiss's car disappeared out of view as it turned at the end of his street.

Bootsie spent the rest of the day lying around the house, he still felt bitter about the previous week's loss and it was a hard pill for him to swallow. He knew all the boys had tried their hardest and the coach was certainly not to blame, he had guided the team to a season with only one loss in the home and away season and that was the first game, that first game was also a loss to the Cobras.

"What do the Central Cobras do differently from us, and why do the Cobras always beat us?" he pondered to himself as he watched TV. Bootsie sat in front of the TV for the rest of the evening watching it but not really seeing it. His mind was elsewhere.

"Ring, Ring!!" The sound was coming from the phone in the hallway. Bootsie tried to ignore it.

"Ring, Ring!!"

"If I pretend I can't hear it I won't have to get up," he thought to himself.

"Ring, Ring!!"

"OK, I'll answer it!" his mum said as she came in from outside, "Don't get up," she said to Bootsie in a sarcastic voice.

"Hello?" she said as she picked up the phone. There was a long silent pause.

"Oh my god that's awful," she said, "When?" his mum asked. "I see, yes, I'll make sure of it, OK then, if there's anything I can do, yes well, OK then. Bye," said his mum in a very quiet tone as she hung up the phone. "Who was that?" asked Bootsie's dad who had come down from upstairs, "Are you OK?" he asked Bootsie's mum, who had turned as white as a sheet.

"No!" she replied.

"What is it?" he asked her knowing something was very wrong.

"It's Mr Butkiss and Chris, they're gone!" she replied as tears began to roll down her face.

Bootsie jumped up from the lounge and headed towards his mum. "What do you mean they're gone. Gone where?" he demanded to know. "I'm so sorry Bootsie, but Mr Butkiss and Chris were in a terrible car accident this afternoon, they've both," she paused.

"Both what?" asked Bootsie, begging her not to say it.

"Died," she whispered in a trembling voice.

"NO!!" Bootsie shouted as his back

slid down the wall and he sat on the floor.

He put his head in his hands and began sobbing.

"They can't be, I was with them today," he cried as he tried to get the words out. "We were talking about winning the grand final together next year, it can't be true," he continued to blubber.

Bootsie's dad picked him up from the floor and embraced him.

"It's OK son, get it out, you let them tears out. Don't hold back," his dad said to him.

Bootsie felt like he had cried a river into his dad's shoulder that evening, he didn't think he had any more tears left in him. Bootsie would soon learn he had plenty more tears inside him.

Over the next few days Bootsie was numb, he felt like he had been kicked in the stomach and couldn't get up from it. He had never known any-one who had died before, even all his grandparents were still alive and they must have been very old.

"Chris was only the same age as me," he said to his mum one day, "and Mr Butkiss is about your age. It's just not fair," he added as he sat at the kitchen table with tears strolling down his face.

Bootsie attended the funeral with his parents a week after the terrible news. He had never been to a funeral before and after this one he never wanted to go to another one again. Bootsie took his grand final trophy and put it on top of Chris's coffin.

"This is for the grand final we didn't get to win," he said as he placed it on top of the coffin. His mum and dad stood next to him and held his other hand.

"Goodbye friends," he said as he walked away from the coffins, tears pouring down his face.

Bootsie spent the rest of the summer mostly at home, he never went to the park with Robbie, didn't go to the beach or to the river, the only place he did go was to the Police Boys Boxing Club. He would punch the bags as hard as he could, he was feeling very angry inside and punching the big leather bags made it feel better. Mr Butkiss's car had been hit by a drunk driver, not long after they had dropped off Bootsie at his house.

Bootsie was mad at the world for what had happened to his coach and his friend, he was also extremely mad at the drunk driver who had caused this. He would punch the bag and imagine it was the drunk driver. Dan's dad knew why Bootsie was at the gym and said it was good for him to get his anger out.

"Get it out son," he would say, "You can't be angry forever; eventually you'll have to accept what's happened. But for now, you punch the anger out of yourself and onto that bag," he told Bootsie.

As the weeks passed, the anger did start to go away. He still thought about Mr Butkiss and Chris every day, but now he didn't feel like crying every time he heard their names mentioned. He had spent so much time at the gym that Dan's dad was trying to get him to take up boxing as a sport; Bootsie had become pretty handy with his fists.

"Only in the gym though boys," Dan's dad would say to them. "Walk away from trouble if you can," he added.

Dan's dad started to sing the boys an old country and western song,

"Promise me son, not to do the things I've done,

Walk away from trouble if you can.

Now it don't mean you're weak, if you turn the other cheek,

Son you don't have to fight to be a man."

He sang at the top of his voice.

"Aagh who was that singer again?" he asked with a curious look on his face.

"Oh' Dad, you're terrible, it's just as well you can box, because your singing is awful," Dan said to his dad.

Dan's dad started to chase him around the ring.

"What did you say to me you cheeky little!!" he said as he tried to grab hold of a much faster Dan.

Watching Dan's dad chase Dan around the ring really made Bootsie laugh. It was the first time he had laughed in weeks. It felt good.

2

Mr and Mrs James
88 Oxid St
North edate
9855

All Kings

The thought of going back to rugby training was something that Bootsie was giving a lot of thought to over his summer break. How would he face up to the fact that Mr Butkiss, who he had so much respect for, and his new teammate Chris, wouldn't be there anymore.

"You've just got to remember the good times you shared together," his mum told him one day.

If Bootsie was having trouble with it all, then words can't describe what Robbie was feeling. Robbie had become very close to Mr Butkiss after his initial resistance to him and his coaching ability. Robbie had found an old Regional rugby poster from the year when Mr Butkiss was the coach. In the photo he was sitting right in the middle of the front row with a huge smile on his face. The poster took pride of place on Robbie's wall above his bed. Robbie's mum was very worried about him, as he hadn't picked up a rugby ball even once during his summer break, and this was not like Robbie. Even Bootsie tried to get him to come down to the boxing club but he wouldn't, he just said he wanted to stay at home on his own.

On most days Bootsie's mum would walk down the street and speak with Robbie's mum to see how Robbie was getting on. As with Bootsie, Robbie's mum said that time was making it easier for him and she soon hoped things would get better for him.

On her return from visiting one day, Bootsie's mum came inside with a letter that had a green, black and yellow logo on the top left hand corner of the envelope. She opened the letter and sat down at the kitchen table as she read it to herself.

Dear Parents,

During this season's Regional rugby games your son was sighted by the school's coaching staff, as a future prospect to play rugby for our school.

There are only two scholarships offered by the college each year, one as an academic scholarship and the other as a sports scholarship. We would like you and your son to attend the school during the next two weeks for a formal interview with a view to offering him a chance for selection for the sporting scholarship. He will be required to undertake an English and Math aptitude test. If after the interview process and aptitude test we feel your son meets our requirements he will be offered a full scholarship to attend our fine school at the start of the new school year.

Our school offers the finest education and sporting programs and we feel it would be of great benefit for your son to attend our school and further his studies in this environment.

Our rugby program is also first class and we feel it would also help your son in his future development of the game. Please contact the school and arrange a time and date where you and your son could attend the school for not only the interview but a full tour of the school and its facilities as well.

Kind regards,
Headmaster: All Kings College.

"I think maybe you should read this as well Bootsie," said his mum as she handed him the letter.

"Whose it from?" he asked.

"Why don't you read it first," she replied.

Bootsie's mum watched her son's facial expressions as he read the letter; she wasn't sure how he would react to it.

"Well?" she said after she felt he had read it more than once.

"All Kings College," he said, "Isn't that a boarding school?" he asked his mum.

"Yes I'm pretty sure it is. Actually I think it's both," she replied.

"Why would I want to go to boarding school?" he asked his mum.

"It's up to you Bootsie; it's a long way from here though, so I guess you would have to board there. Maybe we could go and have a look at least, to see what it's like," she replied.

"I suppose we could go and have a look at it and see. A formal interview sounds a bit scary though," Bootsie said to his mum.

"I guess they just want to make sure they choose the right person for the scholarship. A full scholarship is a very good offer I know it's a very expensive school," she replied.

"Isn't it an all boys school?" asked Bootsie.

"I don't know Bootsie, maybe we should ring and make a time to go down there and have a look so we can all get our questions answered," she said to him.

"OK, let's go and have a look," replied Bootsie.

Bootsie was very pleased when his dad got home from work and he could show him the letter.

"All King's College hey," his dad said after he had read the letter. "Good school. Very expensive though," his dad said.

"It says a full scholarship," added his mum.

"Just as well. Do you know what the fees are at that school?" his dad asked.

"No but I can imagine," she replied.

"How do you feel about boarding?" his dad asked Bootsie.

"Scared," he replied. "I mean it would be very different being away from home," added Bootsie.

"Well it's up to you son, I think it's a great offer, but the decision's yours. We'll definitely go and have a look just for my own nosiness, I want to go and have a look at the place for myself," his dad said to the both of them.

"Is Bootsie moving away?" asked Bootsie's sister.

"Maybe, only maybe, at this stage," his mum replied. "Oh, when you say moving away, it makes it sound awful. My little baby's moving away," she added.

"Mum! I haven't left yet, I might not even like it," he replied.

"Good opportunity for you Bootsie, wish I had an offer like that when I was at school. You don't realize how important a good education is when you're at school, if you can be educated at such a good school I think, well it's up to you, but I think it's a great opportunity for you that's all," his dad added.

"Got to pass the aptitude test and formal interview first," said Bootsie, "They might not even like me," he added.

"They will, they will," replied his mum.

3

1)

1.	2.	3.	4.
650 + 93 ——— 743	37 + 78 ——— 115	23 + 19 ——— 42	62 + 32 ——— 94

5.	6.	7.	8.
91 + 33 ——— 124	55 + 23 ——— 78	10 + 96 ——— 106	94 + 60 ——— 154

9.	10.	11.	12.
50 + 91 ——— 141	10 + 76 ——— 86	78 + 17 ——— 95	77 + 80 ——— 157

2)

Write the fraction of the shape or set that is shaded

6) _____ 7) _____ 8) _____

3)

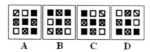

A   B   C   D

"WOW"

All Kings College was about halfway between Bootsie's old house and his new house. His dad had taken a day off work to drive Bootsie and his mum down to the college. As Bootsie and his parents drove down the entrance road into the grounds of All Kings College, Bootsie said one word, "WOW".

"Pretty impressive," his dad added.

"This place is beautiful," said his mum as she looked around the lush green settings of the college.

All Kings College was built in 1899 and had been a school ever since it's opening. For a period after the First World War it was also used as a recovery home for injured soldiers, and it still kept some of its military traditions. It was steeped in such traditions and was probably one of the finest private boys' schools in the region, possibly the country.

"It's like something out of a movie," said his dad as he parked the car out the front of the main building.

Bootsie and his parents were greeted by a member of staff who directed them to be seated outside the headmaster's office and advised them he would let him know they had arrived. As they sat waiting, Bootsie's dad joked that he felt like he was in trouble and was waiting to be told off by the headmaster. As he and Bootsie laughed, the large wooden door next to where they were seated opened and the headmaster of the school greeted them.

"Good morning," he said in a loud confident voice. He was a huge man and was wearing what looked like a black cape.
"You must be the boy they call Bootsie," he said as he shook Bootsie's

hand. Bootsie thought his hand was crushed for sure as he felt the big man's powerful grip.

"Good hand shake, I like that," he said to Bootsie, "And you must be his parents?" he asked, as he shook hands with Bootsie's mum and dad.

"Welcome to All Kings College, have you had a look around yet?" he asked the three of them.

"No not yet, we just got here," replied his dad.

"Plenty of time later," the headmaster added. "I heard you scored a cracking try against that Southern Region last year, young man," said the headmaster to a shocked Bootsie.

"Oh thank you, but it was a team effort," replied Bootsie trying to sound modest.

"Nonsense!" he bellowed, "My scout told me it was a terrible pass and somehow you managed to hang onto it and ground the slippery ball, it was amazing I was told," he continued. "Where did you learn such good ball handling skills?" he asked Bootsie.

"My coach used to put the ball in a bucket of water and detergent at training, he said anyone could catch a dry ball," replied Bootsie.

"What an amazing idea, maybe we should get him down here coaching this team," he said to Bootsie and his parents.

The three of them froze and said nothing.

Bootsie and his parents spoke to the headmaster for about half an hour before Bootsie went to another part of the school and sat his aptitude test. He didn't feel it was too challenging and managed to finish most of the questions in the time limit. While he sat the test, the headmaster continued to talk with his parents in his office.

"I think, if your son is successful, he will be very happy here at All Kings. Good old-fashioned values here, full uniforms including ties and blazers. You don't see that much any more. Good short back and sides haircuts too, no long-haired boys here, I personally make sure of it. He'll be in good hands here, lots of discipline, I'm sure you've already taught him good values and manners and we'll continue to enforce it as well," he told Bootsie's parents as they sat and listened to him.

Bootsie's parents were invited to walk around the school for a look around by themselves while Bootsie went into the headmaster's office alone.
"Well son what are your first impressions of the place?" he asked Bootsie.
"Big," he replied.
"You'll get used to it, have you seen the rugby field yet?" he asked Bootsie.

"No not yet," he replied.

"In time, in time, we'll go and have a look later," continued the headmaster.

"Terrible news about your coach and his son," he said to Bootsie.

He felt his palms start to sweat; he still wasn't overly comfortable talking about it.

"Yes it was terrible," was all he could reply.

"Drink driver, your parents tell me, did the driver die as well in the accident?" he asked a very uncomfortable Bootsie.

"No, the driver walked away with minor injuries," replied Bootsie. "Typical!" replied the headmaster in a harsh voice, "It's always the good ones. We lost a student here last year, same thing, hit by a damn drunk driver. Going home for the holidays the boy was. Very sad times at the school I can tell you," added the headmaster.

"Anyway enough about that let's move onto you, what's your goal in life son?" he asked Bootsie.

"To be honest Sir, I want to play Test rugby, I know I should have a back-up plan, as it's a hard dream to chase, but I believe I can do it and I've always been told if you believe in yourself you can achieve anything," replied a more comfortable Bootsie.

"Good for you," replied the headmaster, "That's the attitude I like to hear. If you do get selected and come here, don't worry, you'll receive the finest education anyway and the world will be at your feet when it's time for you to leave," continued the headmaster.

Bootsie's parents rejoined him and the headmaster in his office, for morning tea together, then the headmaster and one of the housemasters took them on a full tour of the school. They first went to look at the dormitories.

"This is one of the dormitories," said Mr Wood. He had been at the school for many years, first as a student when he was younger, then as a teacher.

"A lot of the teachers here are former students, once you come here, it's very hard to leave," he said to the group as they walked down the dormitory corridor.

"I thought this was a boarding school. Where are all the boys?" asked Bootsie.

"They've gone home for the holidays. We don't keep them under lock and key all year you know," he replied to Bootsie's question.

"You mean I can go home for the holidays?" Bootsie asked.

"Yes, as long as you're back the night before term starts. We also have many four-day weekends during the year so you get to see your family a bit more as well. Don't forget, your family can come down and visit you on weekends as often as they like. It's not a prison," he joked to a relieved Bootsie.

"We are very strict here mind you, lights out at 9.30 pm sharp every night, 10 pm on Friday and Saturday nights. You will have to study between 7.30 pm and 8.45 pm every weeknight except Friday, in silence, at the desk in your cubicle. Breakfast is 7.30am in the dining hall, with school starting at 8.30am until lunch in the dining hall again at 12pm. School recommences at 12.45 pm until 3pm. Dinner is served at 6pm and as I said study commences at 7.30 sharp. All sporting activities take place after school so they don't interfere with the curricular activities."

"We're very academically-based here, if your grade drops lower than what you have scored on the aptitude test today you won't be able to play on any teams, regardless of you being here on a sports scholarship," Mr Wood explained to the group.

"I bet you wish someone had told you about the aptitude test result before you started it hey, I bet you tried your best didn't you?" he asked Bootsie. "Good, because you need a good score to even get in, we base that score on a grade equivalent and like I said, if it drops below that, no sport," he added. "Do any of you have any questions?" Mr Wood asked Bootsie and his parents.

"All sounds very good to me," replied his dad.

Mr Wood said goodbye to Bootsie and his parents and wished him luck in his application. The headmaster walked Bootsie and his parents down to one of the school's ovals.

"Pretty impressive isn't it?" he asked Bootsie and his parents as they stood and looked out on one of the finest rugby fields they had ever seen.

"It's immaculate," said his dad.

"Our grounds keeper prides himself on it, he used to play a bit in his day as well. Here's a tip Bootsie, you can't train or even walk on this field unless it's a game day, it's one of the many traditions here and we're pretty strict about it too," he joked.

The rugby field had a huge grandstand next to it.

"Well Bootsie, can you imagine that packed with people calling out your name?" he asked Bootsie. He didn't let him answer. "Rugby here is our main game, it's a huge thing when the season starts," he added. "We had a few boys selected for the Regional side last year, but they all declined the offer so they could stay and play for All Kings. It's our rivalry with the other schools around here that's the big thing, a very fierce rivalry that goes back a long way," he continued. "Once you're here, you'll find the rivalry between schools is incredible. It makes the Regionals rivalry seem like nothing, you'll see," he added.

The headmaster showed Bootsie and his parents around for a bit longer before wishing them well and saying his goodbyes.
"Goodbye and good luck young man, hopefully you can pull on the green, yellow and black this coming school year," he said as he patted Bootsie on the back. Bootsie had gone to All Kings College not knowing what to expect, now he knew he wanted to be a part of it for sure.

4

The Wait

Weeks had passed since Bootsie attended All Kings College for his interview and aptitude test. He waited for the mail every day hoping he would hear if he had been selected or not.

"Don't get your hopes up too high dear, just incase," his mum said to him.

"I know Mum, I just hope when it gets here, its good news," he replied. Finally one day a letter arrived with a green, yellow and black logo on the envelope. Bootsie ran inside with it.

"Mum, it's here," he shouted as he handed the envelope to his mum.

"Open it then," she replied giving it back to him.

"It's addressed to you and Dad but," he said.

"So, you open it," his mum replied.

"I can't, I'm too nervous, let's leave it till Dad gets home," Bootsie said. "If you want to," she replied.

Bootsie sat and looked at the envelope on the table all afternoon.

"Just open it dear," his mum said.

"No I can wait. Dad wasn't here when I got my regional selection letter and I want him to be here for this one," he replied.

After what seemed forever, his dad walked through the front door of the house.

"Dad, it's here, the letter from the school!" said Bootsie, as soon as his dad walked into the kitchen.

"What did it say?" his dad asked excitedly.

"I don't know. I haven't opened it. We've been waiting for you to get home," he replied.

"Do you want me to open it?" his dad asked.

"Yes, can you read it out loud for me?" asked Bootsie.

"How about if I open it and lay it on the table and we can all read it together," said his dad.

"Good idea," replied Bootsie.

His dad opened the envelope and put the letter on the table.

Dear parents and selected scholar,

"It's good," screamed Bootsie, "It says selected scholar," he added. "Hang on lets read it all first," replied his dad.

We at All Kings College would like to offer your son a full sporting scholarship starting at the beginning of this school year.

"I'm in," said Bootsie in a very excited voice. He didn't read the rest of the letter until later, as he was too busy dancing around the house. His dad continued reading from the letter.

Your son showed exceptional maturity during his interview and scored very highly in his aptitude test. Enclosed is a list of clothing items that will be required for the start of the new school year. Please read the list carefully as strict clothing requirements are to be adhered to at all times at All Kings College.

Your son will be required to attend the College the day before the start of the school year and will be expected to be settled into his dormitory by no later than 5.30 pm on that day, ready for dinner at 6 pm. No dinner will be served to parents on that day and once the boarder is settled, parents are encouraged to leave as early as possible to let the boarders settle in on their own.

Strict rules and guidelines apply at all times at All Kings College and will be strictly enforced. The enclosed book contains the rules and standards expected by students at all times whilst they are a student at the school. You will be expected to know all the rules and standards prior to starting at All Kings.

Once again, congratulations on the scholarship and welcome to All Kings College.

Headmaster: All Kings College.

"Yep you're in. Congratulations!" said his dad.

"Ooh, well done," his mum said, as she gave him a big squeeze. "My baby boy's going off to boarding school," she added.

Bootsie sat down and read the letter over and over; he also studied the 'rules and standards' booklet that came with the letter.

"All sounds pretty normal," he said to his parents. "I wonder what a work party is?"

"A what?" his dad asked.

"It says here, a student who breaks any minor breaches of the school rules or standards will be placed on a weekend work party, further breakage of the rules or standards could result in suspension or expulsion from the school. There are certain matters that will result in immediate expulsion from the school, these matters are known as the six non-negotiable rules," Bootsie replied, as he read from the booklet. "Guess you'll find out if you break the rules. If you broke any of those six rules there though, I'd expect you to be expelled," his dad chuckled, although the look on his dad's face made Bootsie know it was no laughing matter.

Bootsie had four weeks before the start of the new school year; he became very busy getting ready for the start date. He had to buy a lot of clothes including for the first time ever, a school uniform. He had to have grey pants made for him, the school shirts were grey as well and the tie, which had to be worn daily, was the same colour as the school emblem, green, yellow and black. He had to go into town to be measured for the school blazer which was black with the school logo on the left hand top pocket. It also had green and yellow stripes sewn into the two bottom pockets and on the sleeves near the wrist. When they were out in public or for special occasions they had to wear a yellow shirt, tie and the blazer. He also had to wear polished black shoes. When he put all the clothes on at home, his parents were so proud of him.

"You look very smart," they both said.

"How do you feel in it?" asked his dad.

"A bit nervous about it all now it's getting closer," he replied.

"Oh' get the camera," his mum said.

With all the things Bootsie had to get ready for the start of the school year he had overlooked one thing, telling Robbie. Robbie was still getting over the loss of his coach and Chris. It had really impacted on him and he had hardly left the house all summer, now to make things worse, his best friend was moving away as well.

"How am I going to tell Robbie?" he asked his dad.

"You'll just have to tell him," his dad replied. "Hopefully when he goes back to school things will change for him and he can start to put it behind him and move on," he added.

"I haven't forgotten about Chris and his dad yet," said Bootsie.

"Good I'm glad, hopefully you never will. I just mean as time goes by it gets easier and it's easier to move on with your own life. You should always remember them," added his dad.

"I will. I will never forget how good he was to me and the team," replied Bootsie.

"Just go and see Robbie today and tell him. You don't want him to hear it from someone else, do you?" said his dad.

Bootsie walked very slowly up the street to Robbie's house, still not knowing exactly what he was going to say when he got there. Robbie's mum answered the door and welcomed Bootsie inside.

"Bootsie's here," she said to Robbie who was sitting on the lounge.

He looked like he hadn't moved all summer.

"Hi Robbie," said Bootsie, "I've got some news to tell you," he added.

Robbie still didn't say anything.

"I, I've been accepted to All Kings College on a sports scholarship. I leave next week to start there," he said to Robbie and Robbie's mum who still hadn't left the room.

"That's wonderful Bootsie," said Robbie's mum, "Isn't it Robbie?" she asked Robbie, who just reached forward and turned up the TV on the remote control.

"He's still very sad about Coach and Chris," she said as she led Bootsie down the corridor to the front door. "Don't worry about him Bootsie," said Robbie's mum, "He'll be OK in time, you just go away and enjoy you're new school," she said as they walked outside together.

"How was it?" asked his dad when he got home from Robbie's house. "He wouldn't even speak to me," replied Bootsie, "I told him about the scholarship and he just grabbed the remote control and turned up the TV. I just don't understand him," added Bootsie.

"He just needs more time that's all, I'm sure he didn't mean anything by it," replied his dad.

"I hope you're right, Dad," said Bootsie.

"Time heals everything you'll see," his dad added.

5

All Kings College

Scientia est potentia

1
8
9
9

Rugby Union

Life as a Boarder

Before he knew it, Bootsie and his family were packing the car with Bootsie's suitcases ready for the trip to All Kings College. The morning was a happy one as well as a sad one for the family; Bootsie was nervously looking forward to the day but still sad about leaving his home to do so. He knew he had taken a huge step by moving to a boarding school at his age, but he felt that he could handle the big change. Besides he wouldn't be the only boarder at the school, in fact a lot of the boys at the school were boarders.

Just as they were about to leave, Robbie and his mum came down to say goodbye and this pleased Bootsie greatly. Robbie had finally started to get out of the house and start to move forwards, it was just as well considering he had to start school tomorrow. Robbie wished Bootsie good luck and startled Bootsie when he told him he wasn't going to play rugby this year.

"He might change his mind later," said Bootsie's dad as they started the trip south.

The further they got away from his house and the closer they got to the school the more nervous Bootsie got. Sure, he had gone to a four-day Regional's camp last year and an overnight stay during the second Regional game, but he had never really been away from home like this before. It was leaving him with a very nervous stomach.

They arrived at the school just after lunch and Bootsie's dad helped him carry his suitcases. They went into the dormitory that Mr Wood had showed them around, but Bootsie's name wasn't on any of the walls of the cubicles. He later found out this was one of the senior boys' dormitories.

All up, there were twelve dormitories for the boarders and Bootsie's dormitory was called 'McDonald' dormitory. The dormitories were very long with thirty beds on each side. There was a corridor up the middle of the dorm and each boy had his own cubicle. There were no doors on the cubicles. It was all very open with only a head-high partition on either side, this gave each bed and desk a feeling of privacy.

At one end of each dormitory there was a shower and toilet block. The showers were just a massive tiled area with showerheads on the wall about four feet apart. This was a shock to

Bootsie, as he hadn't looked into the showers when they were here last. "Something else I'll have to get used to," he said to himself.

His parents helped him unpack and his mum made his bed for him using hospital corners on the ends, a technique she had learned at nursing school many years ago. Pretty soon Bootsie knew his parents and sister would have to leave and he would be on his own. Well, there would be 360 boys boarding, but with no friends here at all, for the first few days at least, he would be on his own.

The time came for his family to leave, and by this stage of the afternoon most of the boarders had arrived. Bootsie said to his mum, "Please don't cry when you leave, I don't want all the other boys to see you crying."

"I won't," she said, "But you had better write. Do you hear me?" she added. "I put in a pad and some envelopes with stamps already on them; the address is already on the envelopes so you just have to post them. OK?" she said as she felt the tears coming.

Bootsie said goodbye to his parents in the school's car park, and as soon as they got in the car and started the engine, he walked back inside the building to the dormitories. He didn't want to stand there and watch the car with his family in it, drive away without him into the distance. By 5.40 pm all the parents had left, and the dormitory was like a zoo. Bootsie tried to sit at his desk and read a book so it looked like he was busy, covering his nerves at least. A lot of the boys had been boarders the previous year, and were quite settled into college life. Some of the boys had older brothers who also boarded at the school, which made it easier for them to settle in.

At 6 pm Bootsie lined up to enter the dining hall, and when the doors opened, it was a mad rush for a seat. He didn't know where to sit; he had never been here before, he didn't know about the rules and secret codes of the boarders yet, he soon would however. He eventually found a seat and waited for his table's turn to go and collect their meals. He had taken a seat at a table full of older boys. Bad mistake. These boys had been boarders for many years and knew all the rules and codes.

"You have to go and get the meals, Mole," one of the boys said to him, when it was his table's turn to get the trays.
"You're a mole so off you go. Get the trays," said another boy.

Bootsie had to make eleven trips to fetch a tray of food for each boy seated at the table and one tray for himself. He sat and ate very quietly, while the pigs at the table were noisy, and ate like they had never seen food before. They were asking him things like, "Do you want that?" and "If you're not going to eat that can I have it?" each time sticking a couple of fingers on the item of food they were talking about. Bootsie wasn't very hungry and pretty soon had nothing left anyway, after the scavengers at his table had cleaned his plate for him. After dinner he returned to the dormitory and lay on his bed, the full impact of his decision to move here had now dawned on him.

He tried to sleep but with the constant flashing lights of torches and boys running around in the dark all night, it made it very difficult for him to drop off. He was too anxious about what lay ahead, and by the time the last of the night owls stopped running around, he must have fallen asleep about 3am.

"WAKE UP! WAKE UP! I TELL YOU!" a man started to shout in the dormitory. All the fluorescent lights in the dorm were also turned on at the same time. Bootsie opened his eyes, which had only been shut for three hours, to see his housemaster 'Syd'.
Syd was sixty years old and a retired Colonel from the Indian army; he ran his dormitory like he had never left. He had a strong Indian accent still, and Bootsie couldn't really understand what he was shouting about half the time. He was told in no uncertain terms to get out of bed and into the showers. He grabbed what he could find and ran towards the shower block.

Bootsie was still covered in soap when Syd came in.

"Get out, everyone out. Two minutes only, it should only take you two minutes to shower, wash yourself and get out, otherwise you're just wasting the hot water." he barked to the boys. "Next group, in you go," he barked to the boys standing outside. Bootsie realized he had forgotten something in his hurry, a towel. "What are you standing there for?" Syd shouted at him.

"I forgot my towel," replied a very embarrassed Bootsie.

"Well you'd better start jumping up and down until you're dry then," replied an unimpressed Syd.

Bootsie grabbed as many paper hand towels as he could, until he was dry enough and could cover himself before returning to his cubicle to get dressed.

Syd did not let up.

"Get dressed, get dressed," he barked his orders like the boys were Indian soldiers.

"Make your beds, make your beds," he shouted.

"Does he always repeat himself?" Bootsie thought to himself as he tried to dry himself properly, get dressed *and* make his bed.

"Once you're ready, stand in front of your cubicle for inspection. Nobody goes to the dining hall without inspection," he barked again. "Who is this guy?" Bootsie thought to himself as he stood at the foot of his newly made bed, which did not look like it did when his mum had made it yesterday.

Syd walked up and down the corridor inspecting each boy and his presentation.

"Polish your shoes! Your bed is terrible! Tuck in your shirt!" were a few of things he was saying to the other boys.

"Oh my goodness, look at this mess," he said to Bootsie. "Everyone to the dining hall at once," he shouted, "Not you," he said to Bootsie.

All the other boys took off towards the dining hall, and to get away from Syd's inspection.

Syd stayed with Bootsie until he could make a bed how Syd wanted it made. He showed him how he should be dressed and how shiny his shoes had to be each morning. Bootsie also got his first lesson in polishing shoes by Syd. By the time Syd was finished with him and Bootsie finally got to the dining hall, all the other boys were coming back. He found the small service window was shut. No more food. "Welcome to All Kings!!" he thought to himself, as he sat on his perfectly made bed with an empty stomach.

6

Mole Certificate

This certificate certifies you are no longer a mole. It is deemed that you have survived your first year at All Kings and fulfilled all your mole duties, you are now granted the status of no longer being a mole.

If this certificate has cancelled written across it disregard the above as you are considered a mole for life or MFL.

Signed......................
School captain

Get Me Out of Here

The next few weeks were the hardest for Bootsie; his whole way of life was turned upside down. He was slowly getting used to Syd and his no nonsense approach to everything. He could polish his shoes and make his bed to pass inspection every morning, so at least he was making it into the dining hall for breakfast each day. Slowly he was making friends with some of the boys, and once he had told a few boys he was on a rugby scholarship, the other rugby boys started to befriend him.

One boy in particular really helped Bootsie out, 'Razzi'; he had been a boarder at All Kings since the previous year. Bootsie had never heard of where Razzi was born; he spoke with a funny accent and when Bootsie tried to find it on a map one day, he couldn't see it anywhere. His dad was a very important foreign diplomat and Razzi was sent to All Kings for his education and because of the excellent rugby facilities the school had to offer. When his father came to the school, he arrived in a large black stretch limousine. He looked like a very important person. Razzi, like Bootsie was also in the junior rugby team and just like Bootsie was looking forward to the new season.

"You wait till the season starts, you will love it, hey," he said to Bootsie in his strong accent.

Razzi also educated Bootsie on daily life as a boarder.

"What's a mole?" asked Bootsie, "All the older boys call me a mole," he added.

"A mole is a new boy here, you have to do things for the older boys, pol-ish shoes for them and stuff like that. Once you're here for a year and they like you, you get a certificate saying you are no longer a mole. You have to hang it on your wall so they know you're no longer a mole," he told Bootsie.

"What happens if they don't like me?" asked Bootsie.

"Then you get 'cancelled' written across it in black marker pen and you're a mole for life, not a good thing, you'll be polishing shoes forever," Razzi replied.

"It's all tradition, there's lots of funny things like that here, don't worry, it's just a bit of light hearted fun, you'll get used to it. It's great here, you'll see," added Razzi. "Oh yes, and one more thing, stop sitting on the older boys table. You don't have to get their trays for them, they are just using you because you're a mole; you have to try and avoid doing anything to help the older boys. You must sit next to me from now on, Ok?" he told Bootsie.

From the day Bootsie met Razzi, his life at All Kings changed for the better. In the letters he received from his mum, she said he sounded a lot more positive about the school and she wasn't as worried as she first had been with the letters he had been sending home stating how much he hated it.

He grew to know Syd and what was expected of him. He wasn't a grumpy old man; he just wanted his dormitory run properly. If Bootsie wanted advice on anything he could always go to Syd, who was a very quiet and softly spoken man when you got him on his own. He'd been the Indian Army's boxing champion when he was younger and Bootsie soon learnt how well a sixty-year old man could box.

Bootsie managed to keep up with his grades and finally, it was the first day of rugby training. He got changed, and with Razzi, headed down to the oval. He was surprised that the oval the headmaster had shown him was only a game field; they had to train on the training field which wasn't too far from the game field.

"Never walk on the game field unless it's game day," Razzi told Bootsie. "Don't ask me why. It's another tradition here, but if you don't want to upset the headmaster then you'd better stay off it," he continued.

Finally, at training, Bootsie felt like he was doing something he already knew about, there were no secret codes amongst these white lines. The coach was also an ex-Test player who had been to the school as a student many, many years ago and had now returned to give something back. He had played his entire career in the second row and at nearly 6 feet

8 inches, was a huge man. In this country, this guy was a legend.

Bootsie put in a huge first up effort at training; he had now played under many coaches and knew it was important to make a strong first impression. His new coach was aware of who Bootsie was and had heard he had played at the Regional games last year, he also knew he was at the school for his playing ability. Bootsie didn't realize that right from the first training session, a lot was expected from him.

"People are going to look at you and expect you to perform each week without fail," his coach said to him after his first run with the team. "Wait until you see what a game here is like, when the season starts believe me, it gets crazy like a zoo around here," added his coach.

Razzi was the team's number 7; he was an excellent openside flanker and had great speed and power about him. The quality of the other players in the team was also very good; most of the boys here declined selection in the Regional Schoolboys' side in favor of not missing any of the games against the other private schools they competed against.

There was a strong schoolboy competition amongst the other private schools in the Region as well; there were also trips to rival regions to compete against other private schools. Every second year the school sent a team to a different country to compete in a schoolboy's game against similar private and regional school sides. The school also hosted teams from other countries in the year they didn't travel; the school wasn't travelling this year, but instead would be hosting a private school team to stay and play against All Kings.

When it came to rugby at All Kings, nothing was too much, the team had all the best training equipment, including the same scrum machines that the Test team used. During the Test season the Test team or visiting Test teams sometimes stayed at the college and used it as a base camp. The college trophy cabinet was very impressive as well; they had been playing rugby since the school opened in 1899. There were many framed jumpers around the school and pictures of the boys who had played for the school in years gone by.

The rugby players were given old style cloth caps to wear, which were green, black and yellow. Only boys who had actually played a game could wear one. If you sat on the bench for a game and didn't take the field, it meant you didn't get one. It was obviously a great honour at the school to get and wear a cap. Once you earned a cap it was like getting a mole certificate, it meant you had achieved something at the school and you were more accepted by the older boys.

The dormitory was a very different place after Syd went home. He and his wife lived at the college, but in a little house away from the main school.

Syd would return to the dormitory at midnight and 2am like clockwork to check on the boys. The boys knew this, and between those times it was anything goes. Short sheeting a bed was common; the top sheet in the bed gets folded over, so when you tried to get into it your legs only went two feet down the bed. Bed rolling was also common, if you fell asleep too early, or sometimes a late-night birthday surprise, you'd be rolled out of bed, mattress and all. When you woke up in a daze and couldn't work out what the feeling of being squashed was, chances were you'd had your bed rolled. The metal frames of the beds weren't fixed to the ground, so if you slept deeply and woke up still in your bed, but outside, it was because you were carried out there during the night.

Bootsie soon settled into the dormitory experience, he was a rugby boy and although he hadn't been capped yet, he was still known around the school. Another activity the school took on was boxing; Bootsie thanked Dan and his dad for the training, when he was thrown into the ring for a full boxing match one afternoon. All the boys did it at least once during the year and there was no way out of it. Syd ran the boxing club and the school had a full size boxing ring in the gym with rows and rows of seats around it. The gym was better equipped than Dan's dad's Police Boys Club.

Each Friday night was fight night, normally the rugby boys didn't have to fight during the season in case of injuries. But at the moment it was still before the start of the actual season and one Friday night Bootsie had to get in there and box, against Syd!! Although Syd was sixty years old, not one boy could lay a glove on him, including Bootsie.

A boy would get in the ring and try to hit Syd, who would dance around making them look silly. He wouldn't hurt the boys, just give them a bit of a glancing blow when they dropped their guard. Sometimes he would pick boys names from a list, and there would be three bouts every Friday night.

"This place sure is different," thought Bootsie.

7

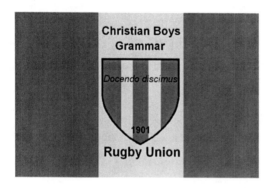

The Zoo

Bootsie's coach had told him the school would be like a zoo when the season started and he wasn't far wrong. The coming Saturday was the opening game of the season and the school had changed accordingly. The dorms were full of boys making green, yellow and black streamers to shake around on game day. The school had its own newspaper, 'The All Kings Gazette' and each week would print out two editions.

Bootsie was interviewed twice during the week by budding future journalists. Even at training the stands were half full, and in the dining hall it was what the boys were all talking about.

Bootsie had befriended Syd, and would go to his house for cups of tea with him and his wife. Boxing was Syd's thing and he wasn't a fan of rugby at all, so it was a nice break, away from all the focus on the game when he was at Syd's house. Syd would tell him about the army and India, while his wife kept feeding Bootsie a constant supply of chocolate biscuits as well as cups of tea. Syd had taken a shine to Bootsie as well, except for in the dormitory where everyone was equal, and not passing inspection still meant no breakfast.

The first game-day finally arrived and the atmosphere of the school lifted again. They were confident of victory. No one considered that losing was an option. The school had two teams, and you couldn't play in your first year unless you were exceptional. The junior team was made up of players from the second and third forms and the senior team had fourth and fifth form boys. Bootsie and Razzi were the only boys in second form who were in the combined age group junior team.

Bootsie would be playing in a grade with boys who were a year older than him.

Both teams had to meet early, down near the practice field and were soon ushered into the change rooms by the coach. They were fully equipped change rooms for the boys and the visiting teams as well. The senior boys' team was allowed to watch the first half of the junior boys' game, but were then expected to be changed and beginning to warm up ready for their own game which followed the junior boys' game.

As Bootsie left the change room and ran onto the field he couldn't believe what had happened. Four large buses had arrived at the school and there was a sea of red and yellow jumpers and ribbons along one complete side of the field. The red and yellow were

the Christian Boys Grammar supporters. In the grandstand and up the entire length of the other side of the field
was a completely different story; it
was a sea of green, yellow and black.

The stand was packed with men some
of whom were quite old but they all
had one thing in common, caps. Every
man who had played at some point
in time for the college was reserved a
seat in the stand. Each of them was
wearing a green, yellow and black All
Kings rugby cap. The headmaster and
the school's teaching staff, except Syd
who was probably at home drinking
tea, were also seated in the stand.
Both schools had chants and songs
they were singing, each group trying
to be louder and outdo the other one.
Bootsie ran onto the field.
"This place *is* a zoo!" he thought to
himself.

Bootsie had never, and I mean never, played a game under such noisy conditions. The hundreds and hundreds of spectators had to stand behind a rope that was three metres back from the touchline and ran parallel with the entire length of the field so the touch judge could run the touchline without tripping over. Bootsie wasn't expecting it to be like this at all, he had played for the Region last year and it was nowhere near like this. This had been happening every weekend for nearly 100 years and he had no idea it had ever taken place before. The opposition drop-kicked the ball very high. The game was on, and the ball was heading straight for Bootsie.

As soon as the ball was kicked, one of the Christian Boys Grammar supporters shouted, "He's gunna!" and then the sea of red and yellow supporters began chanting, "DROP! DROP! DROP! DROP!" until the ball came down to Bootsie, and the unexpected cheering made him completely lose focus on the ball, and it bounced straight off his chest and onto the ground in front of him. He dived onto the ball, hoping there was a hole in front of him he could dive into, and hide for the rest of the game. The crowd was screaming and shouting at Bootsie letting him know what he had done. One boy started to sing, "Oh', show me the boy that can't catch a ball," and then the rest of the crowd joined in as one, "HIM! HIM! HIM!" they pointed at Bootsie, as they sang in their loudest voices.

Bootsie didn't know what to do, he ran so far away from the singing crowd, he forgot he had to come back and take part in the scrum right next to the touchline. As the scrum was about to set, the same boy shouted, "OH', which one's the boy that dropped the ball?" and the rest of the crowd started to point and shout at Bootsie, "HE DID! HE DID! HE DID!" If they did this to put players off their game it had worked. Bootsie was having a shocker.

He was so concerned with the other team's fans he couldn't concentrate on the game. If he missed a tackle, the boy would shout, "OH', show me the boy that can't tackle at all," and the rest would point and shout "HE CAN'T! HE CAN'T! If the team did anything wrong at all, the entire crowd from Christian Boys Grammar had a chant for it. The All Kings spectators were an even louder lot, because they outnumbered the visitors' team's supporters by two to one.

When All Kings had the lineout put in on the Christian Boys side of the field it was a nightmare, the main boy would shout, "OH', show me the team that can't hear the call," and the rest would shout "THEY CAN'T! THEY CAN'T!" It worked too. It was impossible to hear the call, and the players had to use hand signals they had already prepared. Bootsie didn't know any of these signals, and the lineout was a shambles at times on that side of the field. When it was their put-in, it was dead silent, and the same thing happened on the other side of the field with the All Kings supporters.

He was glad of the half-time break. He ran into the change rooms and sat down to try and make sense of the madness that had gone on before him. The score at half time was All Kings 0,

Christian Boys 5, and his coach was not happy at all.

"Boys, boys, boys what's going on out there?" he asked the group. "Not enough heart, you've got to get in there and smash them at the breakdowns, win that ball back. C'mon boys, this is a home game, we've got to win our home games this season. You boys know what away games are like, we've got the crowd on our side today so let's get out there and win back some pride," he said to the group.

As the boys ran back onto the field, the noise from the crowd was unbelievable again. The fly-half on Bootsie's team began kicking the ball to the friendlier side of the field, keeping his players away from the Christian Boys crowd. The noise from the All Kings crowd was far louder than the Christian Boys, and it was all aimed at their players. They were using similar chants aimed at putting the opposition players off their game, Bootsie wasn't used to this at all, and even his own supporters were putting him off his game. It wasn't long before he was replaced by a third-form player.

Razzi played a good game but he had an advantage, he had seen all this the previous year, and Bootsie had wished he had seen it before as well, to prepare him for it. He knew he had played a shocker and really was glad to be taken off. To make things worse, as soon as he was replaced, the All Kings boys scored two trys and the final score stayed as that, All Kings 14, Christian Boys 5.

8

The All Kin

Sunday Edition

SCHOLARSHIP BOYS SHO

Supposed 2nd Form sensation "Bootsie" had a harsh introduction to life as an All Kings player in the match against Christian Boys Grammar on Saturday. From the opening seconds of the game when he dropped the high ball to the shambles at the lineout a headless chicken on the field he was. Thankfully the Coach had the sense to replace him in the second half and Danny from 3rd Form got to play in his usual starting position. From that moment on the game turned on its ear and the junior boys had their first win of the season.

A great effort by the senior team saw them run home convincing winners 34 to 9, more on the senior game in the sports section.

It will be an interesting choice if 'Bootsie' gets the starting 8 position next week when we travel to St Peter's College to take on the blue and whites.

Ren
foll
imp

The
that
rela
the
beh
of a
expr
in li
its
beh
con
or v

It m

The Press

"SCHOLARSHIP BOY'S SHOCKER!" that was the headline in the All Kings Gazette on Sunday morning. Someone had pinned it to Bootsie's wardrobe door during the night. He pulled it down and started to read the story.

Supposed 2nd Form sensation "Bootsie" had a harsh introduction to life as an All Kings player in the match against Christian Boys Grammar on Saturday. From the opening seconds of the game when he dropped the high ball to the shambles at the lineout, a headless chicken on the field he was. Thankfully the coach had the sense to replace him in the second half and Danny from 3rd Form got to play in his usual starting position. From that moment on, the game turned on its ear and the junior boys had their first win of the season.

A great effort by the senior team saw them run home convincing winners 34 to 9. More on the senior game in the sports section.

It will be an interesting choice if 'Bootsie' gets the starting 8 position next week when we travel to St Peter's College to take on the blue and whites.

Bootsie could feel tears building inside his eyes as he read the article; he walked to the toilet and locked himself in a cubicle. He read the paper again, "This is unbelievable" he said to himself as he stood in the toilet. "What do they think I am? A Test player?" he thought. "Do they stay up all night to write this paper?"

Bootsie was shocked. He had been told about what the school was like and it's passion for the game, but this was a whole new level. A few heads poked their way over the top of the cubicle.

"Is he crying?" a voice from the gathered crowd outside asked. "Nearly," said one of the boys who could see Bootsie. Bootsie barged through the door and out of the dormitory. As he left the building he could hear the boys laughing at him.

"Stupid school," he said to himself as he headed for the only safe place he knew; Syd's house.

When Syd answered the door, Bootsie burst into tears.

"Oh my son, what's wrong?" he asked Bootsie. "Come in, come in," he said. "Put the tea on dear," he said to his wife who could see Bootsie was upset. "Now, now," he said, "You tell Syd what's wrong." Bootsie just handed Syd the paper and said, "Look what they wrote about me". Syd read the paper, "Just silly talk," he said to Bootsie as he finished reading the paper.

"Don't you worry about this nonsense; do you think the person who wrote this could play rugby as well as you? No! He could not," said Syd in his thick Indian accent.

"Why did they write it then?" asked Bootsie.

"Silly boy pretending to be a man that's why. Now don't you worry. What you have to do is turn it around on them. You have to get back on the horse and ride it again, and if it throws you off, then you had better get back on it until you can ride the damn thing," added Syd in his animated voice. "Now drink some tea. It fixes everything," he added.

"I couldn't hear myself think and they were pointing and laughing at me," said Bootsie as he sipped his tea.

"You must learn to block out the crowd then," added Syd, "When I boxed, sometimes there were ten thousand people there watching, and half of them wanted me to get my head knocked from my shoulders. If you let the crowd beat you, then you have not done your job. When they shouted for the other man to win, I would fight harder and they soon learned to be quiet. This is what I am telling you to do; you must fight harder and shut that noisy crowd up," said Syd to Bootsie.

Bootsie didn't know if it was the tea or Syd's wonderful advice, but he felt ready to go and face the other boys again. He thanked Syd and his wife, and headed back to the dormitory. It was odd, but when he read the article again, he thought it was quite funny and he was like a star. "Even star players get bad press from time to time," he thought to himself. He looked at his new All Kings rugby union cap, which had been presented to him after dinner the previous night, and thought, "Well I've got something most boys who come here don't ever get."

At training on Tuesday night he was taken aside by his coach.

"What did you think of the zoo on Saturday?" he asked Bootsie.

"It got to me, you know the noise and the chants really put me off my game," replied Bootsie.

"I tried to leave you out there as long as possible, to let you get used to it without it costing us the game. The rest of the boys were awful and they had no excuses, we were very lucky to even get the win. I think it will be a lot easier for you this week, now you've had a taste of private school rugby," he said to Bootsie.

"You are ten times the player Danny from 3rd Form is, and you'll be getting the number 8 jumper this week as well. What did the bad press feel like?" he asked Bootsie.

"You read it?" replied Bootsie.

"Yeah I read it, just for a giggle," added his coach.

"At first I was really upset, but I went and had tea with Syd and he made me feel a lot better about it," Bootsie told his coach.

"Aagh tea with Syd, he's a very wise man and his wife makes wonderful chocolate biscuits," laughed his coach.

"If I had a dollar for every bit of bad press I received, I wouldn't have to do this for a job. Actually I do this for the love of the game and the school, not the money, I made my money playing as a professional," he said to

Bootsie. "Ignore it no matter what they say about you, if you let it get to you they win, and you can't let some soft journalist who's probably never had the guts to pull on a scrum cap, get the better of you. Find out who wrote it and see if he's got any caps in his cubicle, I'll tell you now, the answer is no," he added.

"I've had two bits of advice from two wonderful men today, and it's made me feel like a different person," Bootsie said to himself. He was even able to joke with the other boys in the dormitory later that evening. Deep down he was thinking, "I'll show you lot."

9

St Peter's College

Consilio et animis

1902

Rugby Union

St Peter's

Bootsie wore his new All Kings rugby union cap as often as he could during the week. He even wore it on his way between classes. He left it on his desk during lessons; he wanted the whole school to know he had his first cap, even if it was possibly the worst game he had ever played. He was interviewed on Wednesday afternoon, by what he now called 'boy' journalists, about the upcoming game. He said to the reporter that he had played so poorly because the Christian Boys Grammar supporters were so much louder than the All Kings boys in the crowd. He went on and said he hoped the crowd was going to put on a better performance this week. Talk about taking the heat off him and fighting fire with fire.

In the Thursday edition of the paper, his article was tiny, but there was a huge headline that read, 'All Kings

Boys Show NO Support!' The reporter had taken it upon himself to criticize the All Kings supporters for their lack of passion. Bootsie's plan worked a treat, the heat was totally off him and the reporter faced a backlash of angry boys who demanded he stop writing such things. Bootsie sat back and watched the whole thing unfold before him, he had caused a huge controversy at the school, and by Friday for the first time ever, the paper was reprinted with the headline, 'All Kings Supporters the BEST!' Bootsie read the second edition and thought to himself, "Spineless!"

Saturday morning came, and Bootsie got on the bus with the other players. Being in the team came with privileges, such as the team had its own bus to get them to games. It was a luxury bus as well, compared to the hired buses the non-players, as Bootsie liked to call them, had to travel in. He wasn't being snobbish, he had learned that his critics were all non-players, and not one boy from his team or the senior team had said anything negative to him. Most of them couldn't believe he had never even seen a private schoolboy game before, once they understood this, they all realized why he was put off his game last week.

One good thing about the players' bus was that it was dead quiet, it probably had something to do with the fact the headmaster and all the members of staff rode to the games in it as well.

The supporters from All Kings were piled into four hired buses that followed behind the players' bus. It was like chalk and cheese. In the players' bus you could fall asleep it was so quiet inside. Comparing that to the travelling circus behind them, Bootsie looked back and could see arms and legs hanging out of every window. Each boy was hanging onto green, yellow and black streamers and was waving them to anyone who would look.

It was lucky that they were hired buses and the public didn't know what school they were from. The only bus with a school name on the side of it was the players' bus, which always travelled a good distance ahead of the hired buses. When the public read the name of All Kings College on the side of the players' bus and looked at the quiet and well behaved people on board, they must have wondered what school the circus buses were from. For a school with such strict discipline, they sure turned a blind eye to this.

The buses pulled into the grounds of St Peter's College. Built in 1902, the school's motto in Latin was '*Consilio et animis*' which meant, 'By wisdom and courage.' It was a beautiful school and had a magnificent rugby field to play on. The school colours were blue and white, and the entire grandstand and one complete side of the field was awash with blue and white. The other side, traditionally reserved for the visiting team, was all green, yellow and black. It was also a tradition that no spectator from the visiting team could set foot in the grandstand of the home team. The grandstands at all grounds always have reserved seats for ex-players. These private schools had more traditions than Bootsie could remember.

From the start of the game, Bootsie played better. He couldn't actually play any worse than he did the previous week, as it would have been physically impossible. He caught the ball from the opening kick and ran it straight into the St Peter's defensive line. His powerful run crashed a hole through the defence, and Bootsie ran in and put the ball down under the posts. His first try for All Kings was one of the easiest ever scored by him, and it happened in under thirty seconds. With the try scored and the wind blowing into the stand, the cheering or lack of it couldn't be heard at all, except from the All Kings crowd who had the wind behind them and their voices were being blown across the field and into the St Peter's stand.

Bootsie could hear the All Kings crowd singing, "Which is the team that plays like girls? St Peter's! St Peter's!" He loved it. After the try he was hungry for another one, he wanted to reward the coach for having faith in him and putting him on in the first 15 players. Even though the senior boys were the real first 15, Bootsie thought that if you were given one of the 1 to 15 jumpers, you were in the first 15.

He punished the St Peter's boys with his ferocious tackling in the first half. He chased everything that was near him; it was amazing how the try had fired him up. He picked up the ball off the back of the scrum late in the first half, and charged for the line, he was met by a St Peter's defender and Bootsie almost laughed at his tackle, "If that's all you've got, you'd better get off my field," Bootsie said to himself as he went for the line. With a helping hand from his forwards, Bootsie was over for his second try of the game. Half time score was, All Kings 14, St Peter's 0.

"What a difference a week makes," his coach said at half time, "Great work from Bootsie, that's the sort of effort I want to see out there from all of you," the coach continued. Bootsie didn't really listen; he was on fire and wanted to get back to the action before the fire died down inside him. He was on a mission to prove the boy reporters had totally misjudged him in the previous game.

By his actions in the second half, he proved his critics wrong; he chased down a high kick that the fullback caught inside his 22. The opposing fullback was all by himself in his backline, and didn't shout, "MARK!" The silly boy tried to run around the charging Bootsie, and he was collected and dragged back into his own goal area by Bootsie hanging onto his shirt collar. The referee called for a five metre scrum with All

Kings putting in the feed, the half-back put the ball in, and once again Bootsie picked it up and ran with it. This time he worked the blindside of the field, because the St Peter's boys had stacked the openside and not left anyone defending the blindside. Bootsie ran in for his third try of the game, this one softer than the first. The score was now All Kings 21, St Peter's 0. The score stayed like that until late into the second half.

"Last play of the game boys," said the referee as he awarded the All Kings a free kick. Razzi was smart and took a quick, tapped kick to himself. As he ran at the line, Bootsie grabbed him by his jumper and ran behind him. Bootsie was using Razzi as his battering ram; the poor St Peter's defender, who tried to stop Razzi, got hammered. With Bootsie's extra weight behind, him the defender had no chance and

Bootsie had forced Razzi in for his first try for the All Kings team. After the conversion, it was all over. Final score was All Kings 28, St Peter's 0.

"That's how you silence the press," his coach whispered to him from behind his seat in the bus on the way home. "Great game," he added.

10

The All Kin

Sunday Edition

Scientia est potentia

As our school Motto says "Knowledge is Power" and who ever made the decision to award a scholarship to such a young star certainly has knowledge. Our junior number 8 showed skills beyond his years at yesterday's drubbing of a poor and battered St Peter's team. Bootsie, Bootsie, Bootsie they

cheered as he ran in three tries for himself and used a poor Razzi as a battering ram to help him over the line to score his first try for Kings and a 28 to nil score line for All Kings College.

For a full wrap of the game and all the details of the senior boys win turn to the sports section in the back.

Ren
foll
imp

The
that
rela
the
beh
of a
exp:
in li
its

Knowledge is Power

"Scientia est potentia" this was the headline that greeted Bootsie on Sunday morning as he lifted his tired body out of bed. He reached for the paper, pulled it from his wardrobe door and began to read from the front page.

As our school motto says, "Knowledge is Power" and whoever made the decision to award a scholarship to such a young star certainly has knowledge. Our junior number 8 showed skills beyond his years at yesterday's drubbing of a poor and battered St Peter's team. Bootsie, Bootsie, Bootsie, they cheered as he ran in three tries for himself and used a poor Razzi as a battering ram to help him over the line to score his first try for Kings and a 28 to nil score line for All Kings College.

For a full wrap of the game and all the details of the senior boys win, turn to the sports section in the back.

"Front page two weeks in a row, doesn't anything else happen around here?" he said to himself as he got out of bed and headed for the showers, with a towel this time. "It sure feels nicer when they write nice things about you anyway," he thought to himself as he stood and waited for the hot water to arrive.

When he entered the dining hall every boy in the place stood up and applauded. "How embarrassing," he said to himself as he walked red-faced to his seat next to Razzi.

"I am so sore from when you charged me over the line yesterday," said Razzi to Bootsie.

"You're sore? I think I've broken half my ribs," replied Bootsie, "And I think we killed that St Peter's defender."

Bootsie tried to laugh, but it hurt too much.

"You wait till this week's game against St David's, you think you've seen a zoo here last week, just wait until the St David's nuts arrive here on Saturday," said Razzi to Bootsie as they ate their breakfast.

"Can't wait," groaned a very sore Bootsie.

When Bootsie returned to his cubicle, there was a letter on his bed and he knew what it was without opening it. He sat on his bed and read it to himself.

Dear Student,

Based on your efforts and commitment to the Regional team last year you are invited to attend the Regional Schoolboys selection camp on the 29th of this Month.

If you have any questions or feel at this stage you cannot make it to the selection camp or choose not to take part in the camp, please contact the Regional Schoolboys' rugby office, on the telephone numbers below. If you are interested in attending the selection camp you need to contact the office by telephone in the next seven days after receiving this letter.

Once again we thank you for your efforts last year and we hope to see you at camp this year.

President: Northern Region Schoolboys Rugby Union.

Bootsie was asked by the headmaster to join him in his office during the week and Bootsie knew why.

"Have you responded to the Regional Schoolboys letter yet?" the headmaster asked him as he sat down. This was said in a very different tone from the ones he had heard before.

"No, not yet," replied Bootsie.

"Well what are you going to say to them?" he asked Bootsie quite gruffly.

"I wasn't sure what to do. I was going to ask the coach tonight at training," Bootsie replied.

"What? The coach? Well, I suppose you could ask him, but you should have come to me first," added the headmaster. "Personally I prefer if you stay here and play for the Kings team of course, but I'm bound to say that. We're the only private school that discourages our students from taking part in the games, the regional rugby board is aware of this and they've always kept a very close eye on players from this school. It's not going to hamper your future chances of playing for the region when your time at All Kings is over. They just send out the letters each year in the hope our players will go against the school's policy. The choice is totally yours and I'll leave it up to you," he said to Bootsie as he showed him the door.

"Well that didn't help my decision at all," Bootsie said to himself as he walked back to the dormitory. "I'll ask the coach tonight at training and see what he thinks," he also thought to himself.

His coach wasn't a lot of help.
"What do you want to do?" he asked Bootsie.
"I don't know, and everyone keeps telling me it's my decision to make, I know it is but I just want some advice," Bootsie pleaded.

"I can't tell you what to do Bootsie, it's up to you," his coach replied. "OK, I get it. It's up to me, but at least answer me this, did you play in the Regional Schoolboys competition and if you didn't, did it hamper your entry at all into the Test team?" asked a very frustrated Bootsie.

"I played here for the entire five years of my schoolboy years, I never played Regional rugby even once as a schoolboy. I played more than twenty five times as a senior player though, the board knew who I was when I left here, they contacted me immediately about playing for the senior regional side. When I walked into the pressure of Test rugby it was a breeze, I had already played in front of huge crowds most of which were very hostile and I'd already been booed and jeered at by the best of them. I went on two overseas tours to two different rugby-loving nations. I played against a national under eighteen side here one year and against two touring schoolboy sides as well. When I joined the Test side I watched a lot of great players crumble the first time they were criticized because the critics in the papers got to them and they let them win. I lived in this goldfish bowl for five years and got bad press every second week. Okay, it was only from a journalist writing in a school paper, but as I grew into a Test player, he grew into the senior sports writer for the country's biggest paper. To me it meant nothing, I knew he had never played the game, never earned a cap from All Kings like I had. Do you understand what I'm saying Bootsie?" the coach looked down and asked Bootsie.

"Totally," was all Bootsie could say.

"Play against St David's this week and

then make your decision OK, if you think you were jeered at in the first week, just wait until Saturday," he said to Bootsie, as they began to walk down to the field.

"You stepped on the playing field," Bootsie said to the coach.

"No I didn't," he replied.

"Yes you did, you walked onto it and then realized what you had done and hoped I hadn't seen it," Bootsie quickly said back.

"Yeah well that's a stupid tradition anyway," he replied. The coach put his hand on Bootsie's shoulder and the both of them burst out laughing.

11

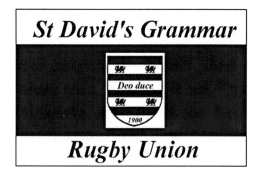

St David's Grammar

Deo duce

1900

Rugby Union

What Are
These For?

Bootsie had no idea what to expect from the visiting St David's team, but by the end of the day, it changed the way he thought of All Kings forever. St David's Grammar school motto in Latin was *Deo duce,* which meant with God as my leader. When All Kings was built in 1899 there was an argument between the two founders of the school as to who would actually be the headmaster at the school. There was a huge court case over the matter and the residing headmaster was awarded the school.

In disgust at the decision the other man used his power in politics to have another much bigger school built the following year. At the time the school offered itself to students with the following statement 'At St David's we offer a much higher standard of education than that on offer at All Kings for *both* boys *and* girls'. Ever since that time the rivalry between the two schools was as big as it gets. In short the two schools hated each other.

They played their first game of rugby against each other in 1901 and this had been the way the argument of which was the better school had been decided ever since then. Whoever won out of the two times each year held the bragging rights for that year, if it was a draw, it was left unsaid until the following game and if both teams won one game each it was called a flat year. St David's had won both games the previous year and it had left a horrible taste in the All Kings headmaster's mouth. He didn't mind losing, just *not* to St David's Grammar.

On Thursday the paper featured an article on what Bootsie's Mum had put in his bacon and eggs to make him so good.

"Really does anything else happen around here?" he had to ask himself. He did cut it out and send it to her, so she could have a laugh as well.

The Friday before the game was bizarre; all the boys carried black and white ribbons and would drop them on the ground, when another student walked by he would step on the dropped ribbon. Bootsie had worked out that St David's school and their rugby team's colours were black and white stripes, but the ribbon thing he just couldn't work out.
"Just another crazy tradition around here I suppose," he said to himself as he watched it happen again and again. After Friday they stopped doing it and the ribbons disappeared as fast as they had appeared in the first place, bizarre!

He went to the boxing on Friday night and watched Syd do his usual display to some poor boys' embarrassment.

"He must have been pretty good in his day," said a boy sitting next to Bootsie, "I've been here three years and never seen a glove laid on him once," the boy added.

Bootsie watched three bouts and then retired to bed waiting for the usual clown antics to begin once Syd left, but they didn't. Out of respect for the players, everyone went to bed and stayed in bed.

"Nice, what about doing this every other Friday night. Thanks," he said to himself as he soaked up the silence.

It was Saturday morning. Game day. Bootsie lay on the bed in his cubicle listening to music and trying his best to relax, he wanted to save all his nervous energy for today's game. After lunch Bootsie and the rest of his team assembled in the changing rooms with the senior boys.

"I'm not going to say anything other than win today boys, because if you don't win, it's all I am going to hear from the headmaster until the next time we play them, so make sure you win!" And that was all he *did* say, to both teams. They knew what to do. WIN!!

As the boys got changed, they could hear by the increase in noise level that the St David's crowd had arrived. St David's had two schools, a boys school and an adjoining girls school, which all came under the same name. The St David's crowd outnumbered the All Kings crowd three to one. Bootsie ran out of the change rooms with the players and his ears nearly exploded, it was indescribable.

"This is only private schoolboy rugby, isn't it today?" he tried to ask one of the other boys.

"What?" was his reply.

It was impossible to hear over the noise. Usually only visiting spectators lined the opposite side of the field to the grand stand. Today the St David's crowd had filled both ends of the field as well as the sideline.

The referee blew his whistle and the madness began. It was a huge opening kick and the ball sailed over all the defending players' heads and rolled into the St David's goal area without touching anyone. The St David's player chose not to ground it or make it dead, but instead he decided he would try and fool the All Kings boys and just pretended to ground it, but didn't actually touch the ground with the ball. As the All Kings players turned their backs on him thinking he'd grounded the ball and that it was either a re-kick or a scrum back on the halfway line, the cheeky player took off, thinking he had fooled them all.

In fact he *had* fooled them all, all except for *one* player. Bootsie saw what had happened and lined him up from when he was still outside the St David's 22. How can a word describe the sound of impact? "Smash!" and "crunch!" don't do it justice. Let's just go with "Woomf!!" Bootsie smashed him.

Want to turn an already hostile crowd against you even more? All you have to do is send the fullback off, injured in the first thirty seconds of the game with a bone breaking tackle, and it's a good start. It was a great tackle. The fullback lost the ball forwards it was jumped on by another St David's player.

"You chose to play on. I saw you put the ball on your foot back there and you didn't ground it. We'll go with the knock on," said the referee. "Scrum to All Kings," he added. From that opening tackle Bootsie was public enemy number one, as far as the St David's crowd was concerned anyway. On the other side of the field and in the grandstand, he was a hero!

The scrum was set right where Bootsie had smashed the St David's fullback, right next to the touchline. The touch judge's ears must have been ringing, as he was standing right next to the crowd and they were screaming at the referee to get Bootsie off.
"It was a good legal tackle, I used my arms and it wasn't high, I got him around his ribcage," Bootsie said to himself, "What's all the fuss about?" he thought. He loved the crowd's

reaction to the tackle, it really fired him up and the louder it got, the better he played.

"Thanks Syd," he thought.

He came off the back of the scrum with the ball in hand and headed infield. It took four St David's players to bring him down. With the arrival of some great support play by the forwards, the ball was passed out to a huge overlap on the wing, and All Kings had their first try of the match. Bootsie couldn't blame the fly half for missing the conversion; the try had been scored right next to the touchline and the poor number 10 had to stand on the touchline and listen to that noise as he tried to kick for goal. It was a terrible kick, and the St David's crowd let him know it. First score, All Kings 5, St David's 0.

It was a close tussle, and by half time the score was still the same, the opposition were a quality team, and deserved their reputation as such a feared team to play. St David's only had enough buses to bring half of their school's supporters to the ground and they still had more supporters than All Kings. Bootsie had heard their home ground was not a nice place for opposition teams. At this stage all that mattered was that the scoreboard showed All Kings were in front, even the headmaster came in to give a speech and fire the boys up. Bootsie realized that this rivalry was bigger than the Regional game from last year. The referee blew his whistle and what seemed like the shortest half-time break ever, was over. The second half was under way.

Bootsie took care of the drop out, no worries at all, he had already learned how to block out the crowd when he wanted to, and he caught the ball no problem. He ran up the touchline, but was tackled into touch before he could go infield. He was being targeted by the St David's players; he was tackled and landed right at the feet of the St David's supporters on the far sideline. He might have been mistaken, but he thought he felt a kick to his leg from a St David's supporter as he got up from the ground. What he *was* sure of was the filthy, disgusting language that was yelled at him when he did get up. He wasn't used to hearing such swear words and this was mostly coming from the girls! He just ran back infield and got on with it.

It was probably the hardest and most brutal game that Bootsie had ever played. It was dirty too, the St David's boys were certainly not playing by the rule book. Bootsie prided himself on being an honest and fair player, but when he kept getting stomped on at each ruck during the game, he wondered how much more he could take. One particular St David's player seemed to be targeting Bootsie; the same St David's player lined Bootsie up and hit him with a very dirty high tackle, Bootsie hit the ground hard. This was like a red rag to a bull. Bootsie did the worst thing a player could do, he retaliated; he got up from the floor, ran over and pushed the St David's player causing him to fall over, right in front of the referee.

The referee saw what had happened and immediately blew his whistle. It was wrong of Bootsie to react like that, because the referee had already seen the high tackle and instead of the St David's boy getting a yellow card and a penalty to All Kings, they both got a yellow card and the penalty was reversed to St David's for Bootsie's reaction.

A yellow card! Since he was six he had played this great game and had never once received a yellow card, he did not like the feeling. He was sent off from the field for ten minutes. He ran over to his coach.
"Just sit down there for ten minutes, we'll discuss it later," said his coach.

Bootsie watched as the St David's players continued to play dirty, although St David's were soon down to thirteen players themselves when the referee had seen enough and finally sent two of their boys off for ten minutes as well.

What horrified Bootsie was that they scored a try five minutes later, with one less player on the field! After an unsuccessful kick, the score was all level at All Kings 5, St David's 5. He watched his sin bin time tick down and when it got down to one minute left, he got up and started to swing his arms to get the blood pumping again. What happened next was the reason Bootsie never played another game of Regional rugby whilst he was at All Kings.

The grandstand, and supporters on the sidelines, erupted as one and started shouting in a deafening voice, "BOOTSIE!, BOOTSIE!, BOOTSIE!, BOOTSIE!"

They kept it up for the whole minute and then some. Bootsie returned to the field and was a machine, he felt he owed the coach and supporters something and was about to deliver it. He went into a ruck and cleaned out two St David's defenders. The ruck collapsed and the ball came out the back of the ruck on the St David's side.

'The ball's out," shouted the referee. Bootsie saw his opportunity and pounced on it. He picked up the ball and ran for the line. He was untouchable and players were bouncing off him. It was as though this moment was what he had trained his whole life for. He powered through the defence, brushing them aside with ease.

"One defender to beat and I'm there," he thought. The poor St David's defender was helpless as he stood there awaiting the raging bull that was approaching at full speed. Bootsie smashed the player backwards, he ran over the top of him and was in at the corner right next to the All Kings supporters, the referee came over, raised his arm and blew his whistle.

"Try!" he shouted.

Bootsie was mobbed by his team and supporters, even the headmaster and the coach were hugging him. He hadn't realized the game was over after the conversion kick had been taken and missed. He was surrounded by so many fans that by the time he could see daylight again, the senior boys were already on the field ready for their game to begin. One St David's supporter ran up, gave him a kiss on the cheek and handed him her name and phone number scribbled on a piece of paper.

Bootsie was carried on the shoulders of the supporters the whole way back to the changing rooms; it had been his greatest rugby moment so far. He was a king, but not of the royal type, he was an "ALL KING"!!

Bootsie soon learned that the whole time his coach had been a student at All Kings, the current headmaster had been headmaster back then as well and was responsible for organizing all those overseas tours and visiting sides coming to the college.

On Sunday, Bootsie was taken to the headmaster's office by his coach. "Bootsie has decided to turn down the Regional camp this year," his coach told the headmaster.
"That's wonderful news, I am so pleased and relieved," he replied. "This school has a lot to offer a young player," he said to Bootsie. "Do you know I was just organising the tour for next year, perhaps you can help me Bootsie," he said, "You too Coach, I could use your help as well," he added.

He reached into his top pocket and pulled out a slim red leather case. He opened it and handed both of them a dart.

"What are these for?" Bootsie asked.

"You'll see," said the coach.

The headmaster shut the door that led to another room in his office. Pinned on the back of the door was a map of the world.

"One dart each. The closest one to a rugby nation and that's where the tour will be next year," his headmaster said.

"Are you kidding?" asked Bootsie.

"Nope this is how I've done it for the last thirty years, son."

Bootsie looked at his coach.

"It's true. I hit where we went to when I was your age, in this very office. The following year we went on tour to the country where the dart landed. The

Regional team's good, but All Kings is better," he smiled down at Bootsie.

They all stood next to each other on a line and the headmaster spoke, "Ready for the tour next year? One, two, three, throw!"

The End.

Check out the Bootsie website
www.bootsiebooks.com

Thanks to KooGa Rugby

www.kooga.com.au

Lightning Source UK Ltd.
Milton Keynes UK
UKOW02f0854021115

261901UK00004B/227/P